MW01177861

Emily Carr

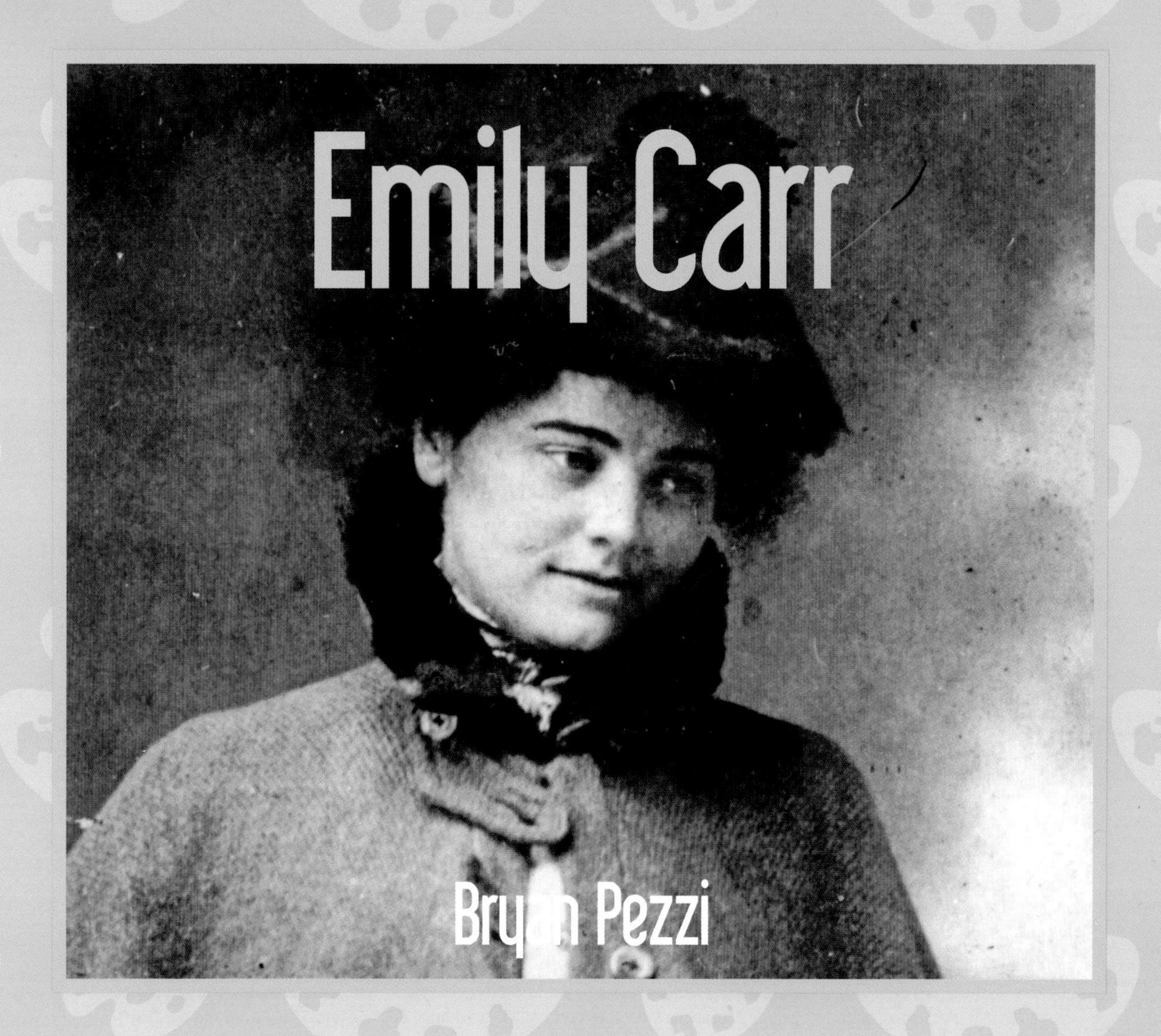

Bryan Pezzi

Weigl

Published by Weigl Educational Publishers Limited
6325 10th Street S.E.
Calgary, Alberta T2H 2Z9
Website: www.weigl.com

Library and Archives Canada Cataloguing-in-Publication Data available upon request.
Fax (403) 233-7769 for the attention of the Publishing Records department.

ISBN 978-1-77071-599-8 (hard cover)
ISBN 978-1-77071-605-6 (soft cover)

Printed in the United States of America in North Mankato, Minnesota
1 2 3 4 5 6 7 8 9 0 14 13 12 11 10

072010
WEP230610

Editor: Aaron Carr **Design:** Kenzie Browne

We gratefully acknowledge the financial support of the Government of Canada through the Canada Book Fund for our publishing activities.

Photo Credits
British Columbia Archives: pages 1 (b-00877), 3 top (f-01220), 3 bottom (a-02037), 5 (d-06009), 9 (a-02037), 12 top (b-09610), 13 bottom (f-01220), 20 (h-02813), 22 left (c-00605); Getty Images: pages 12 bottom, 13 top, 17 top, 17 bottom, 22 right; Arthur Goss: page 15; M.O. Hammond: page 14; Hugh H. McCaughey: page 19 bottom; Bill McLennan, Bill Reid and "The Raven and the First Men," Collections of the UBC Museum of Anthropology: page 19 middle; Ansgar Walk: page 19 top.

CONTENTS

Who is Emily Carr?

Emily Carr is one of Canada's best-known artists. She lived from 1871 to 1945. Carr is known for her paintings of Canada's West Coast. She painted pictures of forests and **totem poles** in British Columbia. Carr's paintings hang in many art **galleries** and museums around the world.

Carr was also a writer. She is known for her stories of the Canadian West. Carr's stories tell what life in Canada was like during her life.

Carr's books have been published in 20 languages. They are sold around the world.

Growing Up

Emily Carr was born on December 13, 1871, in Victoria, British Columbia. She was the youngest of five daughters. She also had a younger brother. Carr's parents moved to Victoria from Great Britain in 1863.

Carr loved to draw and paint from an early age. Her father saw that she had talent. He found an art teacher to give lessons to her. When Carr was a teenager, her parents died. Carr's older sister, Edith, became the head of the house. Carr did not like taking orders from her sister. She wanted to leave Victoria to study art.

British Columbia, Home of Emily Carr

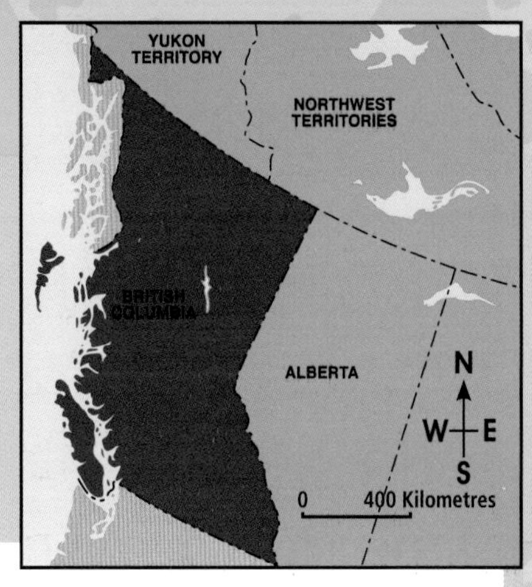

- Carr spent most of her life in Victoria and Vancouver, British Columbia.
- Carr's family home in Victoria is now a museum of her life. People can go there to learn more about Carr.
- Vancouver is home to the Emily Carr University of Art and Design. It is one of the most respected art schools in Canada.
- An **inlet** on the northwest coast of British Columbia is named after Carr.
- The Emily Carr Public Library is in Victoria.

Practice Makes Perfect

After her parents died, Carr spent much of her time drawing. She also wrote in a journal. Later, Carr went to San Francisco to study art. There, she learned to draw with charcoal and paint. Carr spent many hours each day drawing fruit, vegetables, or flowers. She then went to London, England, to continue studying art.

When Carr returned to Canada, she took a job drawing cartoons for a newspaper. She also made money giving art lessons. Carr most enjoyed painting outdoors. She took trips to **remote** areas. There, Carr painted **landscapes** and drew pictures of people she met.

9

Overcoming Obstacles

Carr suffered from health problems for much of her life. She spent more than a year in a London hospital. Doctors told Carr she had to rest. She was not allowed to paint.

Carr did not earn enough money selling her art to support herself. She had to take other jobs to make money. Carr taught art classes. She made rugs, pottery, and other crafts to sell. Carr also owned a small apartment building and rented out the rooms. She even raised Old English sheepdogs to sell.

11

Key Events

In 1899, Carr visited a **First Nations** village on the west coast of Vancouver Island. The people there gave Carr the name *Klee Wyck*. This means "laughing one." Carr drew pictures of the people and their homes.

Carr travelled to France in 1910. She took art classes there. Carr learned a new style of art that used bright colours and big brush strokes.

In 1911, Carr spent six weeks travelling to First Nations villages in British Columbia. She wanted to paint pictures of the totem poles in these villages. Totem poles are made from huge tree trunks. They have human faces and animals carved into them. Totem poles have special meanings. Sometimes, the carvings tell a story.

Carr became ill in 1937. She was too sick to paint. Instead, Carr started writing. She wrote stories about her life.

Influences

In 1927, Carr travelled to Toronto for an art show. There, she met the Group of Seven. These seven Canadian artists worked together and held art shows. They went to many parts of Canada and painted colourful landscapes. Meeting the Group of Seven inspired Carr to paint in her own style. The paintings she made after she met the Group of Seven are thought to be her best.

Carr became friends with Group of Seven member Lawren Harris. He was a **mentor** to Carr.

Achievements and Successes

Carr created her best-known paintings after the age of 57. Art galleries across Canada, the United States, and Europe showed Carr's work.

Carr's first book was called *Klee Wyck*. Parts of *Klee Wyck* were read on the radio in 1940. The book was published a year later. In 1941, *Klee Wyck* won the **Governor General's Literary Award**. This is one of the highest awards a book can win in Canada.

In 1927, Carr had her first major art show. Her paintings were part of a National Gallery of Canada (NGC) art show in Toronto, Ontario. The NGC is known for showing the works of Canada's most important artists.

Carr had a successful art show at the Art Gallery of Ontario in 1937. The show was the first to feature only Carr's paintings.

Carr wrote seven books. Four of them were published only after she died in 1945.

What is an Artist?

Some artists create **sculptures**, **ceramics**, or **prints**. Others, like Carr, use paints and pencils to make pictures. Carr also used words to tell stories. This is another kind of art.

Art can be a hobby or a career. Many artists study art in school. They practise for years to make art they can sell. Many artists have a special style. This makes their art different.

Artists Through History

Like Carr, these artists have achieved success.

Kenojuak Ashevak

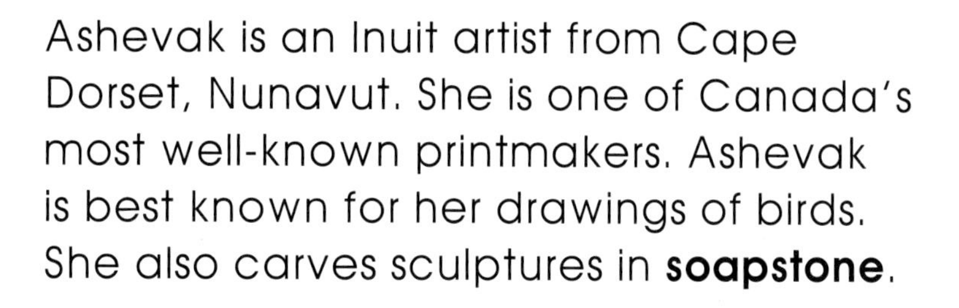

Ashevak is an Inuit artist from Cape Dorset, Nunavut. She is one of Canada's most well-known printmakers. Ashevak is best known for her drawings of birds. She also carves sculptures in **soapstone**.

Bill Reid

Reid was born in Victoria, British Columbia. His mother was Haida. Reid was interested in Haida art. He carved totem poles and huge wooden sculptures. Reid also created sculptures out of metal. His art often shows stories and characters from Aboriginal legends.

Alexander Colville

Colville is an artist from Nova Scotia. He is one of Canada's most successful painters. Colville's paintings show scenes from everyday life. They are very detailed. He works slowly, using thousands of tiny brush strokes.

Timeline

1871	Carr is born on December 13 in Victoria, British Columbia.
1888	Carr's father dies. Her mother died two years earlier.
1899	Carr travels to London, England, to study art.
1910	Carr travels to France to learn a new style of art.

1927	Carr's art is shown at the National Gallery of Canada.
1937	Carr becomes ill. She stops painting and starts writing instead.
1941	Carr makes her last trip to the woods to paint landscapes.
1942	Carr's book *Klee Wyck* wins the Governor General's Literary Award.
1945	Carr dies on March 2 in Victoria, British Columbia.
1966	The last of Carr's seven books is published.

Write a Biography

A person's life story can be the subject of a book. This kind of book is called a biography. Biographies describe the lives of people who have had great success or done important things to help others. These people may be alive today, or they may have lived many years ago.

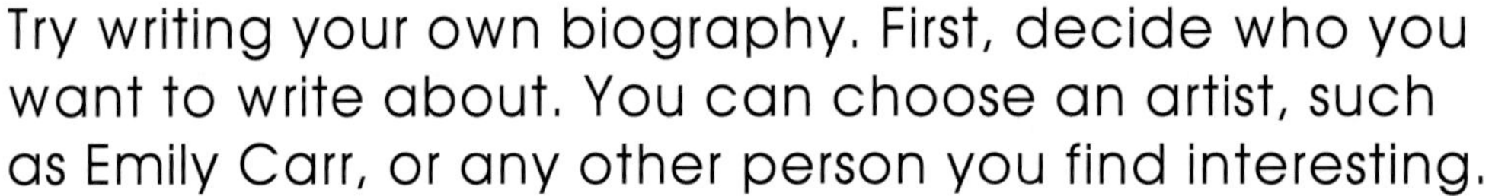

Try writing your own biography. First, decide who you want to write about. You can choose an artist, such as Emily Carr, or any other person you find interesting.

Then, find out if your library has any books about this person. Write down the key events in this person's life.

- What was this person's childhood like?
- What has he or she accomplished?
- What are his or her goals?
- What makes this person special or unusual?

Answer the questions in your notebook. Your answers will help you write a biography.

Find Out More

To learn more about Emily Carr, visit these websites.

See samples of Emily Carr's work at this site.
www.virtualmuseum.ca/Exhibitions/EmilyCarr/en/featured/index.php

Visit this site to see a collection of Canada's totem poles.
www.emilycarr.org/totems/exhibit/index.htm

Learn more about Emily Carr's life at this site.
www.emilycarr.ca

Go to this site to find out more about Emily Carr and her childhood home.
www.emilycarr.com

Glossary

ceramics: bowls, vases, and pieces of art made from clay that is heated until it is hard

First Nations: Canadian Aboriginal peoples who are not Métis or Inuit

galleries: rooms or buildings where works of art are shown

Governor General's Literary Award: an award given to the best books published in Canada each year

inlet: a small bay that is usually long and narrow

landscapes: paintings of outdoor scenery

mentor: a wise and trusted teacher

prints: a design printed onto paper, using ink, a press, and some kind of stamp or plate

remote: far away and hard to reach

sculptures: shaping figures or designs by moulding clay, carving marble or wood, or pouring liquid metal into moulds

soapstone: a soft stone often used for sculpting

totem poles: large tree trunks carved with faces of animals or people; a form of Aboriginal art

Index